SPOTLIGHT ON AN EQUITABLE WORLD

BUILDING CONNECTIONS

Mary Ratzer

ROSEN PUBLISHING

Published in 2025 by The Rosen Publishing Group, Inc.
2544 Clinton Street, Buffalo, NY 14224

First Edition

Editor: Greg Roza
Book Design: Michael Flynn

Photo Credits: Cover Chayantorn Tongmorn/Shutterstock.com; cover, p. 3 (hands) Dedraw Studio/Shutterstock.com; (series Earth icon) v4ndhira/Shutterstock.com; p. 5 Featureflash Photo Agency/Shutterstock.com; p. 6 FloridaStock/Shutterstock.com; p. 7 Andocs/Shutterstock.com; p. 9 lev radin/Shutterstock.com; p. 10 Brendt A Petersen/Shutterstock.com; p. 11 Jamie Hooper/Shutterstock.com; p. 13 wavebreakmedia/Shutterstock.com; p. 14 LightField Studios/Shutterstock.com; p. 15 Nicole Glass Photography/Shutterstock.com; p. 17 Monkey Business Images/Shutterstock.com; p. 19 Drazen Zigic/Shutterstock.com; p. 21 CarlosBarquero/Shutterstock.com; p. 22 dotshock/Shutterstock.com; p. 23 Prostock-studio/Shutterstock.com; p. 25 fast-stock/Shutterstock.com; p. 26 Jacob Lund/Shutterstock.com; p. 27 bangoland/Shutterstock.com; p. 29 Gelpi/Shutterstock.com.

Library of Congress Cataloging-in-Publication Data

Names: Ratzer, Mary Boyd, author.
Title: Building connections / Mary Ratzer.
Description: [Buffalo] : Rosen Publishing, [2025] | Series: Spotlight on an equitable world | Includes index.
Identifiers: LCCN 2023055855 (print) | LCCN 2023055856 (ebook) | ISBN 9781499477290 (library binding) | ISBN 9781499477351 (paperback) | ISBN 9781499477016 (ebook)
Subjects: LCSH: Community life--Juvenile literature. | Social interaction--Juvenile literature. | Communities--Juvenile literature. | Community development--Juvenile literature.
Classification: LCC HM761 .R38 2025 (print) | LCC HM761 (ebook) | DDC 307--dc23/eng/20231218
LC record available at https://lccn.loc.gov/2023055855
LC ebook record available at https://lccn.loc.gov/2023055856

Manufactured in the United States of America

CPSIA Compliance Information: Batch #CSRYA25. For further information contact Rosen Publishing at 1-800-237-9932.

CONTENTS

Empathy Is a Force 4
Sharing More Than a Space. 6
Loneliness Epidemic 8
Creating Community Connections 10
Building Community Schools 12
Welcome Signs 14
Positive School Communities 16
Checking out Relationship Skills. 18
Friendships and Connections Beyond Family . . . 20
Connecting Online. 22
Online Disconnects 24
Active Listening. 26
Conflicts Break Connections. 28
Gratitude 30
Glossary. 31
Index 32

Chapter One

EMPATHY IS A FORCE

If *Star Wars* movies taught generations of fans anything, it was the power of the force. Those heroic characters who had the force could use their will and their special talent to break through barriers and stop evil. The force is awesome, but imaginary. Empathy, however, is real. It uses your will and your special talents. It's definitely a force to connect with others, be an ally to those in need, and build community. Empathy is a tool for building connections.

Communities are where you discover who you are and what gifts you can share. When you become an active part of a community, your self-awareness grows with new experiences and relationships. Values guide choices to take steps outside your comfort zone. Beliefs inspire you to treat others as you would wish to be treated. And in the process of becoming your best self, you use your strengths and talents, your gifts to share with the community. Every small kindness is a gift of yourself.

Young people may find it difficult to make connections and engage in community service. As a pathway to learning how to contribute to your community, students across the United States participate in service education. Guided by their school, students choose among local and real-world opportunities to connect and serve the needs of others. They are mentored by their teachers and adult volunteers already making contributions. Matching interests and strengths with potential service options helps young people to succeed and discover their gifts.

Actor Mark Hamill, also known as Luke Skywalker, has long been involved in charitable organizations, including End Hunger Network, March of Dimes, and Make-a-Wish Foundation. His empathy for others is well documented.

Chapter Two

SHARING MORE THAN A SPACE

Communities both in nature and among people share what scientists call a web of life. This web, like the web of a spider, has hundreds of connecting links that help the members of a community survive. The connections nurture and sustain all. The fact that all members of a community share a common place is just the beginning point. Think about how connections work to support a thriving community. Think about the possibilities when community members connect to work together toward common goals.

If you're a bee, or a plant, or a young person, the community is where you belong. Your community shares food, shelter, safety, and everything you need to grow and develop as a person. Healthy human communities share trust, purpose, and values. These are building

The spider works diligently to create a space, the spider web, that can support it and sometimes its offspring. It's a home, a source of safety, and a way to catch food. How is this like the community you live in?

Local farmers markets are good places to meet and make connections with people in your community. You can buy produce, sell your goods, and network with others.

blocks. Like mutualism in plant and animal communities, members benefit each other with their strengths and resources. They work together, each benefitting the other.

Building communities involves sharing experiences, developing relationships, welcoming differences, and celebrating belonging. Connecting with others who share common interests builds a community. Taking time to get to know those new to a community opens a connection that's likely to grow. Volunteering to contribute your talents and energy to support a community project develops relationships while benefitting others. You belong to many communities, not just your home base. You might engage with a community in a space, but you are always sharing more than a space. You are sharing connections that help many to thrive.

Chapter Three

LONELINESS EPIDEMIC

In 2023, U.S. Surgeon General Dr. Vivek Murthy issued a health advisory warning of an epidemic of loneliness. Americans isolated during the COVID-19 pandemic continued to suffer from loneliness, a trend that had been on the rise for about a decade. The way people interact and talk to each other now, including through online forums instead of in person, leaves about half of Americans feeling lonely. Murthy has concluded that "we are seeing more forces that take us away from one another and fewer forces that used to bring us together."

Studies show that loneliness hurts the health of isolated people as much as smoking 15 cigarettes a day. Physical health and mental health decline without human connections. Seeing this as a public health challenge, Murthy's response includes strategies to reconnect Americans using public parks, libraries, community groups, and a new approach to social media.

Students in school are certainly part of the epidemic. Kids who move frequently and change schools experience isolation when leaving connections and friendships behind. Kids who move to a new school from another country can become isolated because of language and cultural differences. The California Healthy Kids Survey uses data to show that kids feel more socially isolated as they progress from middle school to high school. Many teens experience loneliness and isolation in school, but just one positive relationship with a teacher can make a difference.

Dr. Murthy is the first U.S. surgeon general of Indian descent. He served as an advisor to the COVID-19 pandemic response program under President Joe Biden.

The problem of loneliness is a part of modern life around the world. Lonely people sometimes pull away from others and become quietly separated. Others become angry. Many develop physical or mental health problems. This can be changed.

Chapter Four

CREATING COMMUNITY CONNECTIONS

You can solve problems by creating a small community within a larger one. Isolation and loneliness are challenging problems. How could a welcoming space to connect with others provide solutions? Community centers often open their doors to people who can benefit from connecting with others.

In 2018, 11 people worshipping at a Jewish synagogue in Pittsburgh, Pennsylvania, died when a shooter driven by hate attacked them. Members of the community responded by embracing the families affected. This community concern spread to other states where similar actions affected Jewish congregations. Bonds of support and caring created communities of survivors. Gifts of shared connections sustained those in shock and grief.

Two people comfort each other in front of a memorial after the deadly shooting in Pittsburgh, Pennsylvania.

Loneliness can affect older people, especially those who live alone. Senior citizen centers offer them a place to foster relationships and get involved in fun activities. Many young people choose to be a part of this process.

In the Dallas/Fort Worth area of Texas, citizens formed the Rainbow Garden Club for LGBTQ+ individuals to gather, garden, and make the community a better place to live. Weekly meetings welcomed allies and involved the public library and a local arts organization. This alliance created social support and positive connections.

Senior citizens benefit from senior centers where shared experiences and opportunities can change lives for the better. Lonely people find friendships, social interaction, and a reason to engage with the community. After-school programs for kids are communities with safe, trusting relationships and support. A person's mental health and physical health can improve from relationships and activity with others.

Communities provide physical and mental health to members who engage in shared activities and projects that solve problems for others. People make better decisions when they consider others instead of just themselves. A sense of belonging and being welcomed and valued makes connections stronger.

Chapter Five

BUILDING COMMUNITY SCHOOLS

A community school is a publicly funded school that combines a center of learning with a center for community activities. Sometimes problems are the seeds from which communities grow. The growth of community schools started with thoughtful and committed people who recognized a problem, which was poverty. This problem resulted in numerous negative consequences and stood in the way of learning for those affected. But the problem was bigger than the children. Indeed, it was bigger than the school. The problem was a part of a community that needed equitable opportunities for all students. Schools opened their doors to the greater community and shared solutions for many problems.

One in five jobs in the United States doesn't pay enough to keep a family out of poverty. Children of the working poor sometimes have parents who work more than one job just to make ends meet. When children from other countries arrive at a new school, they could be refugees from war or disasters. For these families, starting over with very little in a strange, new place can be a struggle. They need a helping hand.

Community schools open points of access for many kinds of services. They create a place that's already shared by a community and extend its purpose and capabilities. They provide connections to resources such as clothing, free healthy meals, health care, tutoring, mental health counseling, or other services before, during, and after school. Schools also provide guidance for related community support in one space. These connections can relieve the stress and insecurity that impact kids and their learning.

Community schools help foster a sense of belonging for all people, regardless of their abilities and challenges.

Chapter Six

WELCOME SIGNS

Social isolation affects many people, but it may hit teen students the hardest. Negative posts on social media, a break from groups of friends, or being left out because of differences can isolate students. Strategies to solve this problem, however, might inspire you to think about becoming part of the solution.

Beyond Differences is a student-led project with ties to over 9,000 schools. The purpose of this program is to inspire students to end social isolation and create cultures of belonging. The program trains student leaders in how to engage with students to open conversations about isolation and inclusion. Kids your age commit to ending isolation in schools.

Peer-to-peer encounters encourage students to share their experiences with isolation. It's a good way to battle loneliness.

Sandy Hook Promise is a nonprofit organization that was established to educate kids and adults about gun violence.

Beyond Differences also sponsors No One Eats Alone Day where student volunteers celebrate the power of connecting with others. No One Eats Alone promotes reaching out to fellow students who normally eat alone and ask them to join a group.

The Sandy Hook Promise supports strategies to reduce isolation and build community in schools. After the tragic school shooting there in 2012, parents and leaders have worked to focus on the importance of recognizing and overcoming social isolation. Conversations with peers and reflection builds awareness and community.

Their Start with Hello project teaches students to be more connected to each other. Student mentors work with younger students to raise awareness of isolation and the power of empathy to change it. Instead of judging others, student role models commit to supporting others and take action for inclusion.

Chapter Seven

POSITIVE SCHOOL COMMUNITIES

A positive school climate is one that supports all learners and their academic and social growth. A caring and engaging teacher in every classroom establishes trusting and supportive connections. A teacher that cares and builds relationships can motivate their students to succeed and overcome obstacles. Experts agree that the job of education is a human one based on relationship building.

Positive school communities value the importance of belonging and offer a welcoming climate. They are safe places to learn. Teachers greet students at their doors and keep pathways open for student ideas and communication. Active listening and attention to student voices and choices are an important part of school culture. Students are involved in making decisions and have choices along with responsibility. Connections across lines of difference boost diverse perspectives.

Positive school communities work because they value and foster empathy, respect, self-awareness, and social awareness. They encourage a growth mindset, which means that learners become resilient and continue to work for success. Challenges are a part of learning. Such schools recognize and celebrate students' successes. These communities focus on strengths, talents, and purpose. Expectations are high. Although expectations are high, students are well supported by members of the community.

Guidance couselors are trained to help students with a variety of problems, but they are also trained to be good listeners. They help create a positive school community.

Attention to mental health and well-being provides guidance and support for students who face personal struggles. Taking action to stop and prevent bullying and isolation sustains connections and safety. Expert staff counsels and assists those who need support. Advocates protect and help kids who are at risk.

Chapter Eight

CHECKING OUT RELATIONSHIP SKILLS

Relationship skills grow as children move from childhood to adolescence. By middle school, they've already mastered many relationship skills. As a person interacts with others, they probably don't stop and think, "What relationship skill is this?" Check out some relationship skills used as a part of a healthy life. Relationships are a big part of what is needed to thrive.

Reflect on the examples below. Recognize that you can make an "I can" statement about these skills. "I can" means that you know you have this skill. "I can do this!" Some skills are still to be developed and will become important skills for life.

- **communicate my perspective and listen to the perspectives of others**
- **recognize my role in a conflict and try to prevent conflict**
- **be open to solutions for problems and resolve them when possible**
- **work with others for solutions that work and compromise when needed**
- **advocate for myself and what I need**
- **recognize unhealthy relationships and healthy relationships**
- **seek and offer help and collaborate with others**
- **make good decisions and responsible choices**

You can discuss these statements with your friends. You can work together to make your school community an inviting, inclusive place.

- have strategies to show respect to others and their cultures
- understand what friendship is how to learn from it
- build relationships with people who are different from and similar to me
- be trusted and trust others
- resist negative social pressure
- contribute positively to groups with strengths and talents
- stand up for the rights of others and resist negative social pressure

Chapter Nine

FRIENDSHIPS AND CONNECTIONS BEYOND FAMILY

Friendships and social connections are lifelines to happiness, health, and well-being. This is especially true for middle school students and teens. The feeling of being accepted is key to your mental health and the development of a positive identity. Friendships teach relationship skills that last for life. Learning compassion, caring, and empathy in trusting relationships outside the family opens the door for you to experience new supportive connections for good times and bad.

As the most racially and ethnically diverse generation ever in America, adolescents today have bridged differences to make friends. A large Pew Research Center study in 2018 found that six in ten young people have a close friend that is of a different gender, race, or ethnicity than they are. About half of the pre-teen and teen population have a close friend belonging to a different religion. White, Black, and Hispanic kids are all likely to report that they have a close friend of a different race or ethnic group. Because of connections supported by social media, many friendships are formed despite distance. Friendships can grow from online connections as well as school or neighborhood ties.

Growing up with these diverse relationships means Generation Z will be more prepared than older generations to succeed in a country that is more and more diverse. According to Pew, most members of Gen Z, born roughly between 1996 and 2012, have a positive view of America's growing racial and ethnic diversity.

The population of the United States is diverse. It's made up of many different types of people with many different beliefs, looks, abilities, and cultures. There's no reason we can't all get along and thrive together.

Chapter Ten

CONNECTING ONLINE

Adolescents use digital connections to interact with friends they met in person or through social media. Most young adolescents spend time online with their friends every day. Sharing interests, having fun, and asking questions, young people find common ground in online groups. Many young people report that they've found positive relationships on social media while meeting new people outside their familiar peer group. Openness to differences and evidence of social support can be a part of your online experience.

However, there can be a dark side to spending too much time on social media. Many teens experience negative words and actions and decide to disconnect from others. When teens try to hold onto a place in a peer group, they can experience online pressure, bullying, targeting, isolation, loss of self-worth, and dangers to mental health.

Online forums and chatrooms allow young people around the world to get to know each other and learn about different cultures. The internet can bring people together.

Friendships that start online and not in person are more likely to happen for older adolescents who use social media often. Research on chatrooms, instant messaging, online videogames, TikTok, Facebook, Snapchat, and Instagram shows that these venues stress the importance of easy and quick access to services and actions. The convenience of social media makes it easier for kids to spend time with their friends online instead of in person. Family responsibilities, sports, activities, and transportation limit available time to "just hang out," so online connections fill the gap.

Many are separated by distance from friends and family and depend on online connections to stay in touch. Social media connects families in desperate times. For example, video chat has made it possible for the children of war zones, such as the war in Ukraine, to speak with and see their parents who are involved in the fight.

Chapter Eleven

ONLINE DISCONNECTS

Social media experiences can be positive. It can also be hurtful and harmful. Long hours scrolling on Instagram or TikTok have proven to negatively affect self-esteem, mental health, and relationships. Comparing yourself with others online often leads to despair about status and acceptance. Awareness of the effects of social media is important to your health. Adolescents need to check in with their feelings when online time makes them sad, question their identity, lose self-worth, or experience hopelessness.

This is especially true for middle school students who are still developing confidence about their identity. Sometime, the perfect photographs teens share on social media about their great lives aren't telling the whole truth. Behind the posts could be a person living a real life that is far from perfect.

Cyberbullies purposely target an individual or group to harm them. Bullies gain power through these attacks. Their goal is to cause pain, which they consider to be the reward for their actions. Cyberbullies have a problem with empathy and gain encouragement when others approve of their hurtful actions. This is a personal disconnect from the people they harm.

A 2022 study showed that online bullying has stronger negative effects on a victim's mental health than in-person bullying. Victims suffer depression and anxiety and might even be at risk of taking their own lives. You can disconnect from these experiences by avoiding social media. Sharing your experiences with trusted adults and following their advice is very important.

If you're experiencing cyberbullying, disconnect from the internet for a while and talk to a trusted adult. This could be a parent, aunt, uncle, religious figure, or school counselor.

Chapter Twelve

ACTIVE LISTENING

In the play *Death of a Salesman*, the character Linda Loman desperately reminds her two sons that they need to care enough to connect with their father. Her words are: "Attention must be paid!" Not caring enough to really listen negatively affects our connections with others.

Boredom, lack of interest, distractions, insecurity, or having other things on your mind make listening a challenge. Constantly posting selfies online demonstrates a widespread sense of self-interest that affects genuine attention to others. Has someone said, "I told you that!" But you have no recollection of ever hearing the message? Do you focus on what you want to say next instead of the words someone is sharing in a conversation? Respectful connections depend on listening.

Active listening is an important skill that everyone can benefit from, whether you are a teen or an adult.

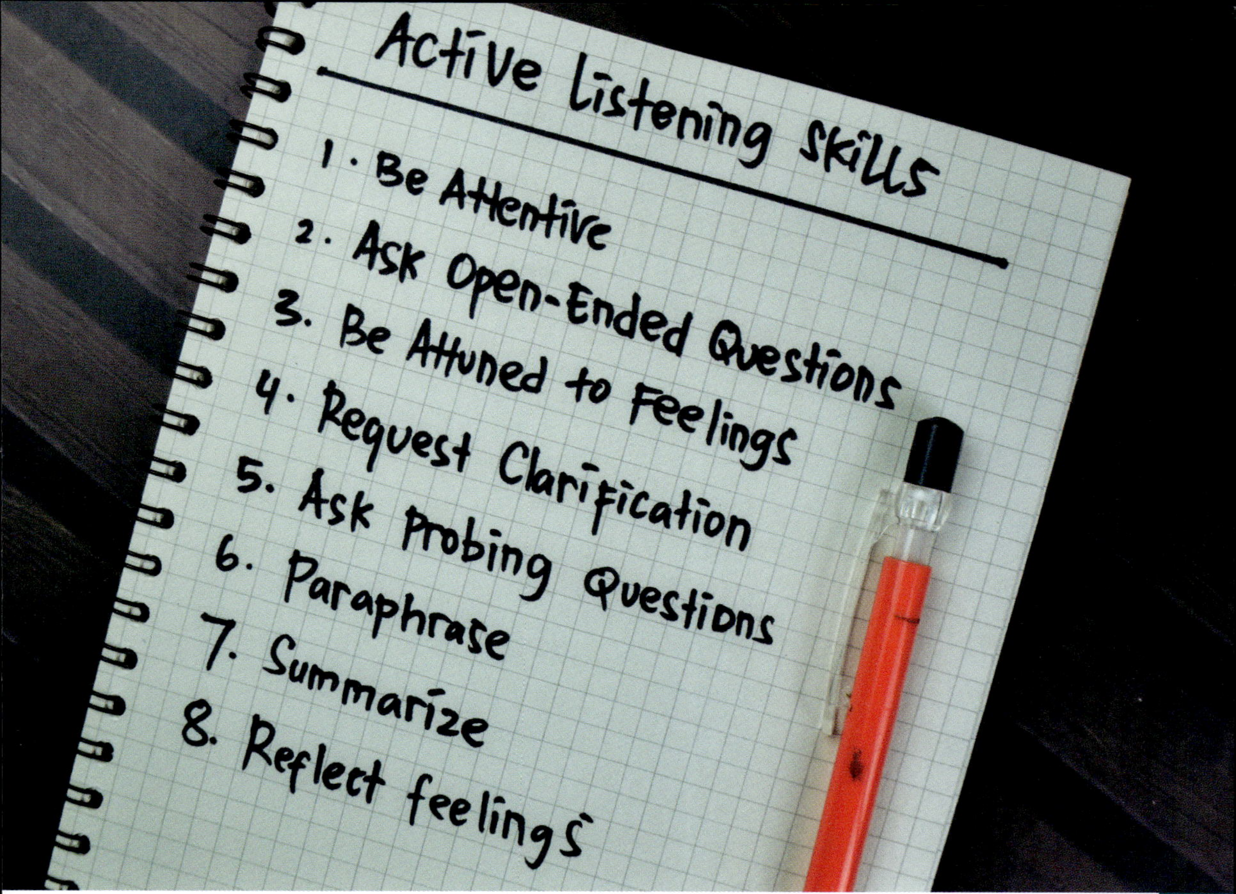

Active listening needs to be learned. It needs practice and awareness. You need to decide to use active listening skills. Connecting positively with others depends on this. You can tell when someone is really listening to you. You can tell when they disconnect.

Try a few easy steps to be an active listener while building a positive relationship. It's essential that the other person knows that you are paying attention and giving them respect. Your facial expression can show interest, compassion, and support. You can use encouraging words of agreement or understanding. Ask questions about what you are hearing. Try to understand clearly what a person is saying and meaning. If the message is complicated, try to summarize to show you are following. Say back what you are hearing. Try saying: "So you are saying . . ." or "I hear you making the point that . . ."

Chapter Thirteen

CONFLICTS BREAK CONNECTIONS

Conflicts are normal but can affect connections between people and their relationships. Learning to handle a conflict situation might take some new skills. Resolving conflicts fairly requires communication, management of emotions, and understanding of perspectives.

Start with ground rules: Try to agree to work together to find a peaceful solution. Agree to avoid name-calling, yelling, blaming, interrupting, or not listening.

Emotions: Be aware of your emotions. Try to stay calm. Anger makes conflicts much harder to resolve. Use self-control to manage your emotions.

The problem: Identify the problem and what the conflict is about. Discuss what is causing the conflict and state what each person wants.

Communicate and share perspectives: Each person explains the dispute from their point of view. Try to be patient and cope. Offer your side of the conflict and stand up for yourself. Staying positive helps. Listen with empathy. Respect the perspectives of the other person.

Find common ground: Find out what facts and issues everyone agrees on. Make clear why different issues are important to each person.

Even the best of friends get mad at each other once in a while. It's important to know how to resolve conflicts. This often brings friends closer together.

Create options: Both sides brainstorm possible solutions and share. Hold back on judging the solutions or the person you're in conflict with. A solution where both sides feel good about the solution is a win for all. Compromise may be necessary.

The solution: A positive and fair solution meets everyone's needs. Agree on a positive option. Give it time to try it out. Discuss whether the solution works and if not, try another strategy. Trust an adult to guide you if needed.

Chapter Fourteen

GRATITUDE

Connecting and belonging to a community can be a positive force in the lives of all. Investing in the social and relationship skills that make your community thrive inspires gratitude in others. Being grateful for the positive experiences and benefits of communities keeps people aware of the power of true connections with others. Relationship skills combined with social awareness create the power to build connections. Experiences, curiosity, open-mindedness, and positive attitudes promote new connections.

Communities are built on all kinds of connections that add to the quality of life for everyone. Social awareness is the ability to understand the perspectives of others and to empathize with others including those from diverse cultures and backgrounds. Socially aware people recognize the strengths in others and choose to respect their feelings. Gratitude comes when people are open-minded and thrustful of others.

A mom in Massachusetts became very sick. As an active and generous member of her community, she shared her talents and gifts with many. Caring for the needs of kids, moms, friends, and strangers, she connected with hundreds of people. In her illness, many stepped up to help her. So many volunteered to make dinners, walk the dog, pick up her kids, do the laundry, clean the house, and drive her to treatment, a complex schedule had to be drawn up on a spreadsheet. This support lasted three years. Gratitude worked two ways.

Every day you can be the person for whom others are grateful. You can be the person who belongs, connects, and is the community with others.

GLOSSARY

alliance: A union between persons, families, or parties that benefits everyone.

ally: A person or group that provides assistance and support in an ongoing effort, activity, or struggle.

anxiety: Fear or nervousness about what might happen.

collaborate: To work together with others, often on an intellectual project.

compromise: An agreement in which each person or group gives up something in order to end a dispute.

consequence: Something that happens as a result of a certain action or set of conditions.

depression: A mental state marked by sadness, inactivity, and loss of a sense of one's own worth.

empathy: The action of being aware of, comprehending, and being sensitive to another's experiences, thoughts, and feelings; also, the ability to share another's emotions.

epidemic: A sickness that spreads widely and affects many people at once.

equity: Fairness or justice in dealings between persons.

mentor: Someone who teaches, gives guidance, or gives advice to someone, especially a less experienced person.

mutualism: An association between people or groups that is beneficial for all parties involved.

pandemic: An outbreak of a disease that occurs over a wide geographic area (as multiple countries or continents) and typically affects a significant proportion of the population

perspective: Point of view.

resilient: Tending to recover from or adjust easily to misfortune or change.

volunteer: To do something without getting paid for it.

INDEX

A

active listening, 26, 27
after-school programs, 11

B

Beyond Differences, 14, 15
bullying, 17, 22, 24

C

community, 4, 6, 7, 10, 11, 12, 15, 16, 17
community center, 10, 11
community school, 12, 13
conflict, 28, 29

D

diversity, 20, 21, 30

E

elderly, 11
empathy, 4, 5, 15, 16, 20, 24, 28, 30

G

gratitude, 30
guidance counselor, 17

H

health, 8, 9, 11

I

isolation, 8, 10, 14, 15, 17, 22

L

loneliness, 8, 9, 10, 11, 14

M

mental health, 8, 9, 11, 17, 20, 22, 24
Murthy, Vivek, 8, 9

R

relationships, 7, 16, 18, 19, 20, 22, 23, 24, 27, 28, 30
respect, 16, 19, 27, 28

S

Sandy Hook Promise, 15
service, 4
social media, 14, 20, 22, 23, 24, 25

T

teacher, 4, 16

V

values, 4, 6
volunteerism, 4, 7, 30